RECOVERY REINVENTED:

THE FIRST 90 DAYS WITH YOUR CLIENT AS A NEW PRS

BY SREA JONES-HARRINGTON

WWW.LETSWRAP.COM

Recovery Reinvented:
THE FIRST 90 DAYS WITH YOUR CLIENT AS A NEW PRS

© 2023 Srea Jones-Harrington

All rights reserved. No part of this book may be reproduced, stored in a retrieval system, or transmitted in any form or by any means, electronic, mechanical, photocopying, recording, scanning, or otherwise, without the prior written permission of the author, except in the case of brief quotations embodied in critical reviews and certain other noncommercial uses permitted by copyright law.

This book is intended to provide helpful and informative material on the subjects addressed. It is sold with the understanding that the author and publisher are not engaged in rendering professional services through this publication. The contents of this book are based on the personal and professional experiences of the author. This book is NOT intended to be used in lieu of seeking professional help and guidance.

The author and publisher specifically disclaim any responsibility for any liability, loss or risk, personal or otherwise, that is incurred as a consequence, directly or indirectly, of the use and application of any of the contents of this book.

For permissions requests and other queries, contact the author at PrettyNerdyG@gmail.com

First Edition: July 2023

CONTENTS

Introduction: Welcome — 06

Chapter 1
Understanding the Role of a Peer Recovery Specialist — 08

Chapter 2
YKnowing Your Client: Building Trust and Understanding — 16

Chapter 3
Creating a Comprehensive 90-Day Plan — 23

Chapter 4
Handling Difficulties and Setbacks in the Early Days — 32

HEALING WITH HEART: YOUR GUIDE TO SELF LOVE IN RECOVERY & BEYOND
BY SREA JONES-HARRINGTON
WWW.LETSWRAP.COM

CONTENTS

Chapter 5 — 42
Therapeutic Techniques for Effective Recovery

Chapter 6 — 52
Fostering Long-term Commitment to Recovery

Chapter 7 — 60
Self-Care and Professional Boundaries for PRS

Conclusion — 69

Message from the Author — 75

ABOUT THE AUTHOR

Meet Srea Jones-Harrington – your guide, mentor, and companion on this journey towards self-love and recovery. Srea is not just a Self-Love Strategist and Registered Peer Recovery Specialist; she's a passionate advocate for nurturing one's inner strength and celebrating the unique beauty within each individual.

Srea's journey into the world of self-love and recovery is rooted in personal experiences, professional expertise, and an unyielding passion to help others rediscover and embrace their inherent worth. Her philosophy is centered on the premise that at the core of recovery lies the power of self-love, and it's this belief that forms the cornerstone of her work.

As the creator of The AFTA Effect: A Six Week Self-Love Leap Bootcamp, Srea has guided countless individuals through the process of acknowledging their past, forgiving their mistakes, trusting in their abilities, and accepting themselves—flaws and all. Her approach goes beyond surface-level changes, focusing instead on fostering deep, transformative self-love. Srea's mission is to help each person realize that they are, indeed, the beholder of their own beauty, possessing the power to shape their journey of recovery and self-discovery.

ABOUT THE AUTHOR CONT...

Srea's work as a Self-Love Strategist involves more than providing guidance. It entails creating a safe, supportive, and empowering environment where individuals feel seen, heard, and valued. Her role as a Registered Peer Recovery Specialist brings a unique, empathetic perspective to her work, allowing her to connect deeply with those she supports.

Srea's commitment to her work is unwavering, born out of a profound understanding of the challenges, triumphs, setbacks, and victories that accompany the journey of recovery. She believes that self-love is the most potent tool in this journey, and through her work, she strives to equip every individual with this tool, empowering them to navigate their path with strength, resilience, and grace.

Throughout this guide, Srea's expert insights, compassionate approach, and unwavering belief in your potential have been a guiding force. Her words are not just advice; they are an invitation — an invitation to embark on the most rewarding journey you'll ever undertake: the journey towards loving yourself unconditionally.

In closing, whether you're at the start of your recovery journey or well on your way, Srea Jones-Harrington is here to remind you of your inherent strength, your boundless potential, and most importantly, your deservingness of self-love. So here's to you, to your journey, and to the power of self-love, guiding you every step of the way.

INTRODUCTION

Welcome to the exciting and rewarding world of a Peer Recovery Specialist (PRS)! Whether you've found yourself here out of a deep-seated passion for helping others, a desire to make a difference, or personal experience with recovery, the road ahead is a fulfilling and profoundly influential journey. As a newly assigned PRS, the first 90 days with your client can set the tone for their entire recovery process. This eBook serves as a comprehensive guide to help you navigate these crucial days confidently and effectively.

Why is this eBook crucial for you? The first 90 days with a new client is a pivotal period. It's during these initial days that trust is built, plans are devised, and groundwork is laid for a successful recovery journey. The knowledge you'll gain from this eBook will equip you to manage this period efficiently, ensuring you're capable of providing the best support for your client's unique needs.

In the upcoming chapters, you'll delve into the critical aspects of being a PRS. Starting from understanding your role, you'll explore how to build trust and understanding with your new client. You'll learn how to devise a comprehensive 90-day plan that caters to your client's specific recovery goals. Recognizing the possibility of early setbacks, we'll guide you on how to handle difficulties, ensuring you're prepared to support your client through thick and thin.

Further on, you'll discover various therapeutic techniques that can enhance the effectiveness of the recovery process. Recognizing the importance of a long-term vision, you'll learn strategies to foster your client's long-term commitment to recovery. Last but not least, because your welfare is crucial to your role as a PRS, we'll discuss self-care and maintaining professional boundaries.

As a PRS, you're the guiding light for individuals journeying through recovery. The role is demanding, but equally rewarding. This eBook is designed to help you navigate this new territory with confidence and poise. By mastering the strategies and techniques outlined in the upcoming chapters, you'll be well-equipped to make a significant difference in your client's life.

INTRODUCTION

So let's embark on this journey together. In the first chapter, we will begin by gaining a comprehensive understanding of the role of a PRS and why it is a key component of the recovery process. Let's turn the page and get started!

Please remember, the journey of recovery is unique to each individual, and this eBook serves as a guide, not a rulebook. It's designed to provide a roadmap for the first 90 days with your client, but you are always encouraged to adapt these practices based on your professional judgment and client's specific needs.

Throughout the book, you'll find actionable insights, pro tips, and practical advice that will help you accomplish your goal – devising a 90-Day plan for assisting a new client in recovery. Together, let's strive to make a difference and inspire change.

CHAPTER I

UNDERSTANDING THE ROLE OF A PEER RECOVERY SPECIALIST

As you embark on your journey as a Peer Recovery Specialist (PRS), understanding your role's essence is the first step. This position is more than a job; it is a commitment, a mission, and a unique opportunity to impact lives profoundly. This chapter offers an in-depth understanding of the role of a PRS, so you're well-prepared to provide the best support for your clients as they journey through recovery.

The PRS: A Bridge to Hope and Healing

The PRS role is complex and multifaceted, requiring a combination of empathy, understanding, knowledge, and guidance. You, as a PRS, act as a bridge between the world of addiction and the realm of recovery. You're a beacon of hope, a motivator, and a mentor, walking side by side with your client through the transformative journey towards sobriety.

Your primary role as a PRS is to empower your clients. You're there to guide, not to direct. You help your clients find the courage within themselves to face their struggles, fight their battles, and reclaim their lives from addiction. Remember, your purpose is not to 'fix' them, but rather to assist them in their path towards self-discovery, self-efficacy, and ultimate recovery.

CHAPTER I

The PRS Toolbox: Skills and Competencies

Several key skills and competencies make a successful PRS. Firstly, strong interpersonal skills are crucial. Building a therapeutic relationship with your clients requires trust, rapport, empathy, and understanding. Good listening skills, patience, and emotional intelligence will greatly enhance your effectiveness in building and maintaining these relationships.

Cultural competency is another essential aspect of your role. Addiction and recovery are influenced by an individual's cultural, social, and personal background. Understanding and respecting these differences is critical in providing appropriate and effective support.

Your role also requires problem-solving skills. A part of recovery involves dealing with life's daily challenges while resisting the lure of addiction. By teaching your clients how to identify, analyze, and tackle these challenges, you'll equip them with a crucial skill for long-term sobriety.

Lastly, a PRS must have knowledge about addiction and recovery. This includes understanding the physical, psychological, and emotional aspects of addiction, knowing about different recovery models, and being familiar with community resources that can support your client's recovery journey.

CHAPTER I

Creating Safe Spaces

An essential aspect of your role as a PRS is creating a safe and supportive environment for your clients. Recovery involves confronting difficult emotions and challenging past experiences. For your client to open up about these experiences, they need to feel safe and validated.

Creating a safe space involves a few key elements:

1. Non-Judgmental acceptance: This means accepting your client's feelings, thoughts, and experiences without criticism. It involves seeing them as a person first, not as their addiction.

2. Confidentiality: Maintaining the privacy of your client's personal information is not only ethically required but also crucial for building trust.

3. Emotional support: Provide reassurance, empathy, and encouragement, especially during the difficult phases of recovery.

4. Validating experiences: Acknowledge the reality of your client's experiences. Validate their feelings and their struggles. This can help reduce feelings of guilt and shame associated with addiction.

CHAPTER I

The PRS's Role in Creating a Recovery Plan

A significant part of your role as a PRS is to assist your client in creating a personalized recovery plan. This involves setting recovery goals, identifying potential obstacles, and defining strategies to overcome these obstacles.

In collaboration with your client, you'll:

1. **Define short-term and long-term recovery goals:** These should be specific, measurable, achievable, relevant, and time-bound (SMART).

2. **Identify potential triggers:** Recognize situations, emotions, or people that may trigger a relapse and devise strategies to manage these triggers.

3. **Plan for cravings**: Cravings are a normal part of recovery. Equip your client with techniques to manage these cravings effectively.

4. **Establish a support network**: Identify key individuals, such as friends, family, or support groups, who can provide support during the recovery process.

5. **Integrate self-care:** Ensure that self-care activities are included in the recovery plan to help manage stress and promote well-being.

CHAPTER I

TBuilding Resilience: The PRS's Role in Encouraging Growth

Recovery is not a linear process; it has its ups and downs. As a PRS, you're there to help your client navigate these challenges. You will encourage your client to view setbacks not as failures, but as opportunities for learning and growth. By fostering resilience, you can help your client stay committed to their recovery journey, even in the face of adversity.

To conclude, your role as a PRS is multifaceted and profoundly impactful. You are a guide, a mentor, a confidante, and an advocate. By understanding your role and honing the necessary skills, you can be a pillar of support for individuals journeying towards recovery. Remember, the work you do is invaluable - it brings hope, fosters change, and transforms lives. In the following chapter, we will delve into the crucial aspect of building trust and understanding with your new client.

You're already on your way to making a significant difference. Let's move forward and continue to deepen our knowledge and skills to support your clients effectively.

Know Your Role

CHAPTER 1 QUIZ: UNDERSTANDING THE ROLE OF A PEER RECOVERY SPECIALIST

1. WHAT IS THE KEY ADVANTAGE OF BEING A PRS?

   A. MEDICAL EXPERTISE
   B. PERSONAL EXPERIENCE WITH RECOVERY
   C. LEGAL AUTHORITY
   D. ALL OF THE ABOVE

2. WHAT QUALITY IS NOT CRUCIAL FOR A PRS?

   A. EMPATHY
   B. PATIENCE
   C. IMPULSIVENESS
   D. RESPECT

3. WHAT DIFFERENTIATES A PRS FROM OTHER PROFESSIONALS IN THE RECOVERY FIELD?

   A. THERAPY QUALIFICATIONS
   B. LAW ENFORCEMENT
   C. SHARE PERSONAL EXPERIENCES
   D. NONE OF THE ABOVE

4. WHAT DOES THE PRS-CLIENT RELATIONSHIP CENTER AROUND?

   A. AUTHORITY
   B. POWER
   C. CONTROL
   D. EQUALITY

Know Your Role

Practical Exercises for YOU and your CLIENT

Peer Exercise: Write a mission statement for your role as a PRS. Include your purpose, values, and the impact you aim to make. Reflect on this regularly to stay aligned with your role's core purpose.

Client Exercise: Invite your client to share their expectations of your role. Use this as an opportunity to clarify the boundaries of your role and foster an open dialogue.

Ready to take your journey of self-love and recovery to the next level? I'm here to help! If you're interested in a one-on-one session with me, please reach out at PrettyNerdyG@gmail.com. Let's dive deeper into your unique journey and build on the foundation you've started here.

Alternatively, if you're looking for a structured, immersive program, consider signing up for "The AFTA Effect: A 6 Week Self Love Leap Bootcamp". This transformative program will provide you with additional tools, insights, and support to enhance your journey towards self-love and recovery.

Visit www.LetsWRAP.com for more information or check out my Linktree at Linktr.ee/PrettyNerdyG to explore all available resources and offerings.

CHAPTER 2

KNOWING YOUR CLIENT: BUILDING TRUST AND UNDERSTANDING

Now that you have a profound understanding of your role as a Peer Recovery Specialist (PRS), the next vital step is getting to know your client. Building trust and understanding with your client lays the foundation for an effective and transformative recovery journey. This chapter delves into the importance of building these vital connections and offers actionable steps to achieve them successfully.

The Core of Recovery: Trust and Understanding

Trust is the bedrock of the PRS-client relationship. It's the primary ingredient for creating a supportive, non-judgmental, and empowering atmosphere. The process of recovery demands vulnerability, honesty, and often, the confrontation of painful past experiences. To navigate these challenges, your client must trust that you will provide a safe, understanding, and encouraging environment.

Understanding your client, in turn, is equally critical. Every person's experience with addiction is unique, shaped by their personal history, cultural background, and coping mechanisms. By striving to understand these nuances, you can tailor your approach to best fit your client's needs, thereby significantly enhancing their recovery process.

CHAPTER 2

Building Trust: A Journey of Patience and Persistence

Building trust with your client is a journey, not a destination. It is a process that requires time, patience, and a lot of active listening. Here are some actionable strategies to help you cultivate a trust-filled relationship:

1. **Demonstrate Empathy:** Empathy is your ability to understand and share the feelings of another. It means being able to 'put yourself in their shoes.' By expressing empathy, you signal to your client that they are seen, heard, and understood.

2. **Maintain Confidentiality:** Trust is impossible without confidentiality. Assure your client that their personal information and shared experiences will remain confidential.

3. **Show Consistency:** Consistency in your behavior and approach reassures your client of your reliability. This involves honoring your commitments, showing up on time, and maintaining a steady demeanor.

4. **Encourage Open Communication:** Create an environment where your client feels comfortable sharing their thoughts, fears, and experiences. Encourage them to ask questions and express their concerns.

5. **Validate Their Feelings:** Acknowledge your client's emotions and experiences without judgment. This validation can help reduce feelings of shame and isolation associated with addiction.

CHAPTER 2

Getting to Know Your Client: A Path of Discovery

Getting to know your client is a multifaceted endeavor. It goes beyond knowing their history of substance abuse; it's about understanding their life story, their strengths and weaknesses, their hopes and fears, their goals and dreams. Here are some strategies to gain a deeper understanding of your client:

1.**Encourage Self-Expression:** Provide opportunities for your client to share about their experiences, thoughts, and feelings. This could involve discussions, journaling, or expressive arts.

2.**Learn About Their Background:** Understanding your client's cultural, social, and personal background can provide invaluable insights into their experiences and perspectives.

3.**Identify Their Strengths:** Every person has unique strengths and abilities. Identifying these can help you tailor the recovery plan to build upon these strengths.

4.**Understand Their Goals:** Ask about your client's goals for recovery. What do they hope to achieve? How do they envision their life after recovery?

5.**Recognize Their Triggers:** Identifying potential triggers for substance use can help in devising effective coping strategies.

CHAPTER 2

Harnessing Trust and Understanding: The PRS Approach

Building trust and understanding is not a one-time task, but an ongoing process. As a PRS, your approach should consistently reflect these principles in every interaction with your client. By creating a safe and supportive environment, you can motivate your client to engage fully in the recovery process, explore their emotions, confront their fears, and foster positive change.

Incorporate these strategies into your everyday practice. Remember that small actions can make a significant impact. A simple gesture of understanding, a word of encouragement, or the patience to listen can go a long way in building a trust-filled and understanding relationship with your client.

Trust and understanding aren't just crucial for the therapeutic relationship; they're also powerful tools for recovery. By fostering trust and understanding, you empower your client to confront their challenges, believe in their ability to change, and take active steps towards recovery.

In the next chapter, we'll be diving into the specifics of creating a comprehensive 90-day plan. This roadmap will be built on the foundation of trust and understanding you've established with your client and tailored to their unique recovery journey.

CHAPTER 2

Harnessing Trust and Understanding: The PRS Approach

As a PRS, you've taken on a monumental responsibility, but remember, you're not alone in this journey. Your patience, persistence, and dedication are making a significant difference in someone's life. Let's continue this journey together, step by step, towards a path of recovery and transformation.

CHAPTER 2 QUIZ: KNOWING YOUR CLIENT: BUILDING TRUST AND UNDERSTANDING

1. WHAT IS AN ESSENTIAL STEP IN BUILDING TRUST WITH YOUR CLIENT?

   A. SHARING ALL YOUR PERSONAL EXPERIENCES
   B. KEEPING CONSISTENT COMMUNICATION
   C. MAKING PROMISES ABOUT RECOVERY
   D. TELLING THEM WHAT TO DO

2. WHY IS UNDERSTANDING YOUR CLIENT'S BACKGROUND IMPORTANT?

   A. TO JUDGE THEM
   B. TO TAILOR THE RECOVERY PLAN
   C. TO SATISFY CURIOSITY
   D. TO GOSSIP ABOUT THEIR PAST

3. WHY IS CONFIDENTIALITY VITAL IN BUILDING TRUST WITH YOUR CLIENT?

   A. IT ALLOWS FOR THE SPREAD OF PERSONAL INFORMATION
   B. IT CREATES A SENSE OF SAFETY AND RESPECT
   C. IT'S NOT IMPORTANT
   D. IT GIVES THE PRS POWER OVER THE CLIENT

4. WHICH OF THE FOLLOWING SHOULD NOT BE CONSIDERED WHEN UNDERSTANDING YOUR CLIENT'S BACKGROUND?

   A. THEIR PAST MISTAKES
   B. THEIR STRENGTHS AND WEAKNESSES
   C. THEIR GOALS FOR RECOVERY
   D. THEIR TRIGGERS

Practical Exercises for YOU and your CLIENT

Peer Exercise: Reflect on a situation where someone showed trust and understanding towards you. How did it make you feel? Use these insights to improve your interactions with your client.

Client Exercise: Engage your client in a 'Getting to Know You' exercise. Ask open-ended questions about their hobbies, strengths, challenges, and aspirations. This can foster mutual understanding and build a strong rapport.

CHAPTER 3

CREATING A COMPREHENSIVE 90-DAY PLAN

AEquipped with a deep understanding of your role as a Peer Recovery Specialist (PRS) and a solid foundation of trust with your client, it's time to journey into the next pivotal stage - creating a comprehensive 90-day plan. This roadmap serves as a guiding light, illuminating the path of recovery for your client during the crucial first days of their journey. It is unique, adaptable, and personalized, focusing on your client's specific needs, goals, and aspirations. This chapter offers actionable strategies to create a robust and effective 90-day plan.

The Power of a 90-Day Plan

SIn the realm of recovery, the first 90 days are often filled with intense emotions, substantial challenges, and significant adjustments. A 90-day plan provides structure during this tumultuous period, guiding your client through these challenges and empowering them to take control of their recovery process. It sets the stage for long-term success by establishing recovery goals, identifying potential obstacles, and crafting strategies to navigate these hurdles.

CHAPTER 3

Creating a Comprehensive 90-Day Plan: A Step-by-Step Guide

In the realm of recovery, the first 90 days are often filled with intense emotions, substantial challenges, and significant adjustments. A 90-day plan provides structure during this tumultuous period, guiding your client through these challenges and empowering them to take control of their recovery process. It sets the stage for long-term success by establishing recovery goals, identifying potential obstacles, and crafting strategies to navigate these hurdles.

Creating a Comprehensive 90-Day Plan: A Step-by-Step Guide

1.**Define Clear Goals:** Start by defining the recovery goals with your client. These goals should be specific, measurable, achievable, relevant, and time-bound (SMART). Short-term goals could involve managing withdrawal symptoms, attending counseling sessions, or building healthy coping mechanisms. Long-term goals might focus on maintaining sobriety, improving relationships, or enhancing quality of life.

2.**Identify Potential Triggers:** Triggers are specific cues that could lead to cravings or relapse. They can be people, places, emotions, or situations that remind your client of their past substance use. By identifying these triggers early on, you can help your client devise strategies to manage them effectively.

CHAPTER 3

3.Establish Healthy Habits: Recovery isn't just about abstaining from substance use; it's also about cultivating healthier habits. This might involve regular exercise, a balanced diet, adequate sleep, mindfulness practices, or engaging in recreational activities. Encourage your client to incorporate these habits into their daily routine.

4.Create a Support Network: A strong support network can provide emotional reinforcement during the recovery process. This could include family, friends, recovery groups, or mentors. Help your client identify who they can turn to during difficult times and encourage them to reach out when they need support.

5.Plan for Potential Setbacks: Recovery is often non-linear, with its ups and downs. Prepare your client for these potential setbacks and reiterate that they're a part of the process, not a failure. Discuss strategies to manage these setbacks and return to the path of recovery.

6.Regular Check-Ins: Schedule regular check-ins to monitor your client's progress, address any challenges, and adjust the plan as necessary. These can be daily, weekly, or monthly, depending on your client's needs.

7. Celebrate Success: Recognizing and celebrating progress, no matter how small, can boost your client's confidence and motivation. Encourage them to acknowledge their achievements and use them as stepping stones towards their long-term recovery goals.

Implementing the 90-Day Plan: The PRS Approach

As a PRS, your role is to guide your client in implementing their 90-day plan. Encourage them to take ownership of their recovery process while reassuring them of your unwavering support. Be flexible and open to adjustments. The recovery journey is unique to each individual, and the plan should be adaptable to accommodate your client's changing needs.

Remember, the 90-day plan is not a rigid checklist, but a flexible guide. It's about progress, not perfection. Mistakes and setbacks do not indicate failure, but provide valuable lessons and opportunities for growth.

In the subsequent chapter, we'll explore how to manage the inevitable difficulties and setbacks that may arise in the early stages of recovery. Through these challenges, your client's resilience will grow, further reinforcing their commitment to recovery.

CHAPTER 3

As a PRS, your guidance, patience, and support during these initial 90 days can profoundly impact your client's recovery journey. Let's continue to use our skills and knowledge to empower our clients, facilitate their growth, and guide them towards a brighter, substance-free future. Together, we are making a difference. Let's keep moving forward, one step at a time, on this path of recovery and transformation.

CHAPTER 3 QUIZ: CREATING A COMPREHENSIVE 90-DAY PLAN

1. What does a 90-day plan include?

a) Only a list of therapy sessions
b) Just the client's daily schedule
c) Clear goals, coping strategies, support network, and plan for setbacks
d) A rigid, inflexible regimen.

2. What principle should recovery goals adhere to

a) Vague
b) Unrealistic
c) SMART (Specific, Measurable, Achievable, Relevant, Time-bound)
d) Overwhelming

3. What is the role of the client in creating the 90-day plan?

a) The client should be passive and accept whatever plan the PRS creates
b) The client should actively participate in setting goals and identifying coping strategies
c) The client's role is irrelevant
d) The client should make the entire plan themselves

CHAPTER 3 QUIZ : CREATING A COMPREHENSIVE 90-DAY PLAN

4. What is the importance of identifying potential triggers in the 90-day plan?

a) To shame the client
b) To develop strategies to manage these triggers
c) To make the client feel guilty
d) None of the above

5. How should the 90-day plan be adjusted?

a) It should never be adjusted
b) It should be adjusted only at the end of the 90 days
c) It should be adjusted based on progress and feedback
d) It should be adjusted daily

Practical Exercises for YOU and your CLIENT

Peer Exercise: Draft a mock 90-day plan, considering all the elements discussed in the chapter. Practice refining and tailoring it based on different hypothetical client scenarios.

Client Exercise: Involve your client in creating their 90-day plan. Allow them to set their own goals, identify potential triggers, and devise coping strategies. This encourages active involvement and ownership of their recovery journey.

Ready to take your journey of self-love and recovery to the next level? I'm here to help! If you're interested in a one-on-one session with me, please reach out at PrettyNerdyG@gmail.com. Let's dive deeper into your unique journey and build on the foundation you've started here.

Alternatively, if you're looking for a structured, immersive program, consider signing up for "The AFTA Effect: A 6 Week Self Love Leap Bootcamp". This transformative program will provide you with additional tools, insights, and support to enhance your journey towards self-love and recovery.

Visit www.LetsWRAP.com for more information or check out my Linktree at Linktr.ee/PrettyNerdyG to explore all available resources and offerings.

CHAPTER 4

HANDLING DIFFICULTIES AND SETBACKS IN THE EARLY DAYS

IThe journey of recovery is often not a straight path; it comes with its twists and turns, ups and downs. The early days of recovery can be particularly challenging as your client navigates through withdrawal symptoms, grapples with cravings, and relearns how to live without substances. As a Peer Recovery Specialist (PRS), your role is to guide and support your client through these difficulties and setbacks, reminding them that each challenge is a step forward in their recovery journey. This chapter will provide actionable strategies to help you navigate these challenging times with your client effectively.

CHAPTER 4

Understanding Difficulties and Setbacks

Difficulties and setbacks are an inevitable part of the recovery process. They can come in many forms, including:

1. **Physical withdrawal symptoms:** These can range from mild discomfort to severe health complications, depending on the substance of addiction.

2. **Emotional upheaval:** Clients may experience heightened emotions, mood swings, anxiety, or depression as they adjust to life without substances.

3. **Cravings:** Intense desires to use substances can be triggered by various factors and can make the recovery process challenging.

4. **External pressures:** This could be social pressure to use substances or challenging life circumstances that trigger the desire to escape through substance use.

Recognizing these difficulties as normal parts of the recovery process can help you support your client through them. Instead of viewing these setbacks as failures, treat them as opportunities for growth and learning.

CHAPTER 4

Strategies for Handling Difficulties and Setbackss

1. **Normalize the Experience:** Let your client know that it's normal to experience challenges during recovery. This can reduce feelings of shame and failure, which can often compound the difficulty of the situation.

2. **Revisit the Recovery Plan:** When setbacks occur, it's a good time to revisit the 90-day recovery plan. Do the goals need to be adjusted? Are there new triggers that were not identified before? Revisiting the plan can ensure that it stays relevant and effective.

3. **Teach Coping Strategies:** Equip your client with effective coping strategies to manage their cravings, emotions, and stressors. This could include mindfulness techniques, distraction strategies, problem-solving methods, or relaxation exercises.

4. **Foster Resilience:** Encourage your client to view difficulties and setbacks as opportunities for growth. Foster a growth mindset, emphasizing that each challenge overcome strengthens their resilience and commitment to recovery.

5. **Provide Ongoing Support:** Be there for your client, especially during tough times. Your presence, understanding, and reassurance can be a significant source of strength for your client.

CHAPTER 4

Strategies for Handling Difficulties and Setbackss

6. **Celebrate Progress:** Despite the setbacks, it's important to recognize and celebrate progress. This can boost your client's motivation and confidence.

7. **Leverage the Support Network:** Remind your client of the support network they've built. Encourage them to lean on this network during challenging times.

The Role of the PRS in Handling Setbacks

As a PRS, you play a vital role in helping your client navigate through difficulties and setbacks. Your understanding, patience, and reassurance can make a significant difference in how your client perceives and handles these challenges. Always remind them of their strengths, achievements, and progress to maintain their motivation and confidence.

Remember, setbacks are not a sign of failure, but a part of the recovery journey. They offer valuable insights and opportunities to learn, grow, and strengthen commitment to recovery. In the next chapter, we will explore different therapeutic techniques to further aid your client's recovery process.

CHAPTER 4

Your unwavering support during these challenging times can make a significant impact on your client's recovery journey. As a PRS, you are making a difference, transforming challenges into opportunities, and paving the way towards a healthier, happier life. Let's continue this journey, one step at a time, on this path of recovery and transformation.

CHAPTER 4 QUIZ: HANDLING DIFFICULTIES AND SETBACKS IN THE EARLY DAYS

1. How should a PRS view setbacks in recovery?

a) As failures
b) As a regular part of the recovery process
c) As a reason to give up
d) As a reflection of their performance

2. What is one effective approach to managing setbacks?

a) Ignoring them
b) Blaming the client
c) Criticizing the client d) Using them as learning experiences

3. Why is resilience important in managing setbacks?

a) It helps blame the client for setbacks
b) It helps foster a negative mindset
c) It helps the client persevere and recover from setbacks
d) None of the above

CHAPTER 4 QUIZ: HANDLING DIFFICULTIES AND SETBACKS IN THE EARLY DAYS

4. How should PRS react to a client's setback?

a) With anger and disappointment
b) With empathy and support
c) By ignoring it
d) By ending the professional relationship

5. Why is it important to leverage the client's support network during setbacks?

a) To spread the blame
b) To ensure the client has multiple sources of support
c) To avoid dealing with the setback
d) None of the above

Practical Exercises for YOU and your CLIENT

PPeer Exercise: Reflect on a personal setback or difficulty. How did you handle it? What did you learn? Use these insights to empathize with your client's struggles and provide effective support.

Client Exercise: Work with your client to develop a 'Setback Response Plan.' It should include the steps they should take when they face a setback, such as contacting their support network, practicing a calming technique, or revisiting their reasons for recovery.

Ready to take your journey of self-love and recovery to the next level? I'm here to help! If you're interested in a one-on-one session with me, please reach out at PrettyNerdyG@gmail.com. Let's dive deeper into your unique journey and build on the foundation you've started here.

Alternatively, if you're looking for a structured, immersive program, consider signing up for "The AFTA Effect: A 6 Week Self Love Leap Bootcamp". This transformative program will provide you with additional tools, insights, and support to enhance your journey towards self-love and recovery.

Visit www.LetsWRAP.com for more information or check out my Linktree at Linktr.ee/PrettyNerdyG to explore all available resources and offerings.

CHAPTER 5

THERAPEUTIC TECHNIQUES FOR EFFECTIVE RECOVERY

After successfully navigating the challenges and setbacks that come with the early stages of recovery, the journey takes a turn towards adopting therapeutic techniques to facilitate an effective recovery. As a Peer Recovery Specialist (PRS), it's your role to guide your clients through this process. Familiarity with a range of therapeutic techniques can be instrumental in supporting your client's recovery, as these techniques provide the tools needed to deal with cravings, manage stress, and foster healthier habits. This chapter offers an overview of key therapeutic techniques and how to incorporate them into your client's recovery plan.

CHAPTER 5

Therapeutic Techniques: The Building Blocks of Recovery

Therapeutic techniques play a crucial role in recovery by equipping your client with the skills and strategies to maintain sobriety, manage their emotions, and build a healthier lifestyle. Let's delve into some of the most effective therapeutic techniques for recovery.

1.**Cognitive Behavioral Therapy (CBT):** CBT is a form of therapy that focuses on the connection between thoughts, feelings, and behaviors. It teaches individuals to identify and challenge negative thought patterns and develop healthier responses. For your clients, this could involve identifying triggers, managing cravings, and coping with stress.

2.**Mindfulness-Based Techniques:** Mindfulness involves staying present and aware without judgment. Mindfulness-based techniques, such as meditation and mindful breathing, can help your clients manage stress, reduce cravings, and improve their overall mental well-being.

CHAPTER 5

Therapeutic Techniques: The Building Blocks of Recovery

3.**Motivational Interviewing (MI):** MI is a counseling method that helps people resolve their uncertainties and find the internal motivation to change their behavior. As a PRS, using MI techniques can help you boost your client's motivation for recovery and reinforce their commitment to change.

4.**Relapse Prevention Techniques:** These techniques focus on recognizing the early warning signs of a potential relapse and developing strategies to avoid or cope with them. This could involve identifying triggers, developing coping strategies, and creating an emergency action plan.

CHAPTER 5

Applying Therapeutic Techniques: A Practical Guide

Now that we have explored some key therapeutic techniques let's discuss how you can incorporate them into your client's recovery process.

1. **CBT Techniques:** Use CBT techniques to help your client identify negative thoughts or beliefs that may contribute to their substance use. Teach them how to challenge these thoughts and replace them with healthier ones. For instance, if a client believes they need substances to cope with stress, help them identify this thought, challenge its accuracy, and replace it with healthier coping strategies.

2. **Mindfulness Techniques**: Introduce mindfulness techniques to your client as a tool to manage cravings and stress. Start with simple practices, such as mindful breathing or mindful eating. Gradually, you can guide your client towards more complex mindfulness exercises.

3. **MI Techniques:** Incorporate MI techniques into your conversations with your client. Encourage them to talk about their reasons for change, their hopes for recovery, and their plan to achieve it. Use open-ended questions, affirmations, reflections, and summaries (OARS) to strengthen their motivation for change.

CHAPTER 5

4. Relapse Prevention Techniques: Work with your client to develop a personalized relapse prevention plan. This should include recognizing their personal triggers, developing coping strategies, and identifying people or places they can turn to for immediate support during a crisis.

Therapeutic techniques are an integral part of the recovery process. However, it's important to remember that each client is unique, and what works for one might not work for another. Be open to trying different techniques and find what works best for your client.

In the upcoming chapter, we will discuss how to foster a long-term commitment to recovery. By employing the therapeutic techniques learned in this chapter, your client will be well-equipped to maintain their sobriety and build a healthier, happier life.

CHAPTER 5

As a PRS, you play a crucial role in guiding your client through this journey. Your dedication, patience, and understanding are making a significant impact. Let's continue to use our skills and knowledge to empower our clients, facilitate their growth, and guide them towards a brighter, substance-free future. Together, we are making a difference. Let's keep moving forward, one step at a time, on this path of recovery and transformation.

CHAPTER 5 QUIZ: THERAPEUTIC TECHNIQUES FOR EFFECTIVE RECOVERY

1. What therapeutic technique focuses on the connection between thoughts, feelings, and behaviors?

a) Yoga
b) Meditation
c) Cognitive Behavioral Therapy
d) Dance therapy

2. Motivational Interviewing aims to:

a) Persuade the client to follow the PRS's advice
b) Find the client's internal motivation to change their behavior
c) Force the client to commit to recovery
d) None of the above

3. Why is it important to choose a suitable therapeutic technique for each client?

a) Each client responds differently to therapeutic techniques
b) To overwhelm the client
c) To make the client reliant on therapy
d) All techniques work for all clients

CHAPTER 5 QUIZ: THERAPEUTIC TECHNIQUES FOR EFFECTIVE RECOVERY

4. How does Mindfulness-Based Techniques assist clients in recovery?

a) By increasing stress
b) By teaching them to ignore their feelings
c) By helping them manage cravings and reduce stress
d) None of the above

5. What's the purpose of using Motivational Interviewing in recovery?

a) To persuade the client to follow the PRS's advice
b) To foster the client's internal motivation to change their behavior
c) To let the PRS take control of the recovery process
d) None of the above

Practical Exercises for YOU and your CLIENT

Peer Exercise: Familiarize yourself with various therapeutic techniques by attending workshops or webinars. Practice these techniques yourself to gain firsthand experience of their benefits.

Client Exercise: Teach your client a basic mindfulness technique, such as mindful breathing. Practice it together during your sessions and encourage them to practice it independently during times of stress or craving.

Ready to take your journey of self-love and recovery to the next level? I'm here to help! If you're interested in a one-on-one session with me, please reach out at PrettyNerdyG@gmail.com. Let's dive deeper into your unique journey and build on the foundation you've started here.

Alternatively, if you're looking for a structured, immersive program, consider signing up for "The AFTA Effect: A 6 Week Self Love Leap Bootcamp". This transformative program will provide you with additional tools, insights, and support to enhance your journey towards self-love and recovery.

Visit www.LetsWRAP.com for more information or check out my Linktree at Linktr.ee/PrettyNerdyG to explore all available resources and offerings.

CHAPTER 6

FOSTERING LONG-TERM COMMITMENT TO RECOVERY

Recovery is not just a short-term endeavor; it's a lifelong commitment to health, wellness, and personal growth. As a Peer Recovery Specialist (PRS), one of your pivotal roles is fostering your client's long-term commitment to recovery. This commitment is the driving force that propels them forward, fuels their resilience in the face of adversity, and keeps them anchored on their path of sobriety. This chapter provides actionable strategies to nurture this long-term commitment to recovery.

**The Lifelong Journey:
Long-term Commitment to Recovery**
The journey towards recovery extends far beyond the initial 90-day plan. It's a continual process of self-improvement, growth, and adaptation to a substance-free life. Long-term commitment to recovery is what helps your client maintain the gains made during the early stages of recovery, equipping them to navigate future challenges and transitions without resorting to substance use.

CHAPTER 6

Strategies to Foster Long-Term Commitment

1.**Reinforce the Benefits of Recovery:** Remind your client of the positive changes they've experienced since starting their recovery journey. This could be improved health, mended relationships, increased self-esteem, or a renewed sense of purpose. Highlighting these benefits can reinforce their commitment to maintaining these positive changes.

2.**Encourage Lifelong Learning:** Recovery involves continually acquiring new knowledge and skills. Encourage your client to continue learning about addiction and recovery, to seek new coping strategies, and to stay updated on the latest research. This mindset of lifelong learning can keep them engaged and committed to their recovery journey.

3.**Maintain Regular Check-Ins:** Even after the initial 90-day period, continue to check in with your client regularly. These check-ins provide an opportunity to monitor progress, address any emerging challenges, and reinforce the importance of sustained commitment to recovery.

CHAPTER 6

Strategies to Foster Long-Term Commitment:

4. Set New Goals: As your client achieves their initial recovery goals, help them set new ones. These could relate to their personal development, career, relationships, or health. Having goals to work towards can give them a sense of direction and purpose, bolstering their commitment to recovery.

5. Foster a Supportive Community: A strong, supportive community can significantly reinforce your client's long-term commitment. Encourage them to stay engaged with support groups, recovery events, or sober activities. This sense of community can provide continual motivation, support, and encouragement for the long haul.

6. Empower Your Client: Empowerment is a powerful motivator for long-term commitment. Remind your client that they have the power to shape their recovery journey, and celebrate their accomplishments. This feeling of empowerment can bolster their confidence and determination to stay committed to recovery.

CHAPTER 6

Nurturing Commitment: The PRS Approach

As a PRS, you play a pivotal role in fostering your client's long-term commitment to recovery. Be their cheerleader, celebrating their successes, big and small. Be their mentor, guiding them through challenges and helping them learn and grow. Be their support, reminding them of their strength, resilience, and ability to overcome adversity.

Long-term commitment to recovery is not just about maintaining sobriety; it's about embracing a new way of life—a life of health, wellness, growth, and fulfillment. In the following chapter, we will delve into the importance of self-care and professional boundaries for PRS. You, as a PRS, also need to maintain your wellbeing to continue being an effective guide for your clients.

Your dedication, empathy, and unwavering support are invaluable in this journey of recovery. Let's continue to foster change, empower our clients, and inspire hope. Together, we are making a difference. Onward, we move in this journey, each step leading towards a brighter, healthier future.

CHAPTER 6 QUIZ: FOSTERING LONG-TERM COMMITMENT TO RECOVERY

1. What is one way to foster long-term commitment to recovery?

a) Making recovery a short-term goal
b) Focusing on negative consequences
c) Reinforcing the benefits of recovery
d) None of the above

2. Why are regular check-ins important even after the 90-day period?

a) To monitor the client's every move
b) To control the client's life
c) To monitor progress, address challenges, and reinforce the importance of sustained commitment
d) To make sure the client is dependent on the PRS

3. What's the benefit of setting new recovery goals as initial goals are achieved?

a) It gives the client a sense of direction and purpose
b) It makes the client feel overwhelmed
c) It's not beneficial
d) It allows the PRS to take control

CHAPTER 6 QUIZ: FOSTERING LONG-TERM COMMITMENT TO RECOVERY

4. Why is it essential to maintain regular check-ins even after the 90-day period?

a) To keep the client dependent on the PRS
b) To monitor the client's every move
c) To monitor progress, address challenges, and reinforce the importance of sustained commitment
d) To keep the client busy

5. How does a supportive community foster long-term recovery?

a) It allows the client to forget about recovery
b) It provides continuous motivation, support, and encouragement
c) It is not necessary for long-term recovery
d) It helps the PRS control the client's life

FOCUS ON THE LONG

Practical Exercises for YOU and your CLIENT

Peer Exercise: Reflect on a long-term commitment you've made in your life. What strategies helped you stay committed? How can you apply these insights to foster your client's long-term commitment to recovery?

Client Exercise: Help your client create a 'Recovery Vision Board.' This should include their long-term recovery goals, their reasons for recovery, and images or quotes that inspire them.

Ready to take your journey of self-love and recovery to the next level? I'm here to help! If you're interested in a one-on-one session with me, please reach out at PrettyNerdyG@gmail.com. Let's dive deeper into your unique journey and build on the foundation you've started here.

Alternatively, if you're looking for a structured, immersive program, consider signing up for "The AFTA Effect: A 6 Week Self Love Leap Bootcamp". This transformative program will provide you with additional tools, insights, and support to enhance your journey towards self-love and recovery.

Visit www.LetsWRAP.com for more information or check out my Linktree at Linktr.ee/PrettyNerdyG to explore all available resources and offerings.

CHAPTER 7

SELF-CARE AND PROFESSIONAL BOUNDARIES FOR PRS

Throughout this guide, we've focused on how you as a Peer Recovery Specialist (PRS) can effectively support your client on their recovery journey. However, to continue being an effective PRS, it's essential to maintain your wellbeing and set professional boundaries. This final chapter will explore the importance of self-care and professional boundaries for PRS, offering actionable strategies to ensure you can continue to support your clients without compromising your health and wellbeing.

Self-Care: An Essential Component of Effective Support

Working as a PRS can be emotionally demanding. The weight of supporting others through their struggles can take a toll on your mental and emotional health. That's why self-care isn't a luxury for a PRS—it's a necessity. Self-care ensures that you remain physically, mentally, and emotionally healthy, enabling you to provide effective support to your clients.

CHAPTER 7

Self-Care Strategies for PRS

1.**Physical Health:** Regular exercise, a balanced diet, and sufficient sleep are fundamental to your physical health. Make sure these are part of your routine.

2.**Emotional Health:** It's crucial to find healthy outlets for stress, such as hobbies, meditation, or spending time in nature. Consider seeking support from a therapist or counselor if you find yourself overwhelmed by work-related stress.

3.**Social Connections**: Maintain strong relationships with family and friends. Social connections can offer much-needed support and relaxation.

4.**Professional Development**: Continue your education and training in the field. It can help maintain your motivation and passion for the work you do.

5.**Boundaries:** Set boundaries to ensure you have time for relaxation and personal pursuits outside work.

CHAPTER 7

Professional Boundaries: Key to a Healthy PRS-Client Relationship

Professional boundaries help define the relationship between you and your client. They protect both you and your client by clarifying what is acceptable behavior and interaction within the professional relationship. Setting clear professional boundaries helps prevent burnout, stress, and the risk of ethical issues.

Strategies for Establishing Professional Boundaries

1.**Clear Communication:** From the onset, communicate to your client about the professional nature of the relationship. Discuss the limits of your role and the expectations of behavior from both sides.

2.**Set Work-Life Boundaries:** Define your working hours and communicate these to your clients. Avoid engaging in work-related activities outside these hours to maintain a healthy work-life balance.

CHAPTER 7

Strategies for Establishing Professional Boundaries

3.**Avoid Dual Relationships**: Do not enter into multiple relationships with a client (e.g., as a friend, business partner, or romantic partner). Such relationships can lead to conflicts of interest and harm the professional relationship.

4.**Emotional Boundaries**: While empathy is crucial in your role as a PRS, avoid becoming overly emotionally involved in your client's experiences. Maintain a level of emotional detachment to prevent emotional drain and burnout.

5.**Seek Supervision**: Regularly consult with a supervisor or mentor to discuss any challenges or concerns related to professional boundaries.

Remember, establishing and maintaining professional boundaries isn't about creating a wall between you and your client. It's about creating a safe, effective, and ethical professional relationship that respects both you and your client's needs.

CHAPTER 7

The journey you've embarked on as a PRS is not just about supporting your client; it's also about maintaining your health, growth, and wellbeing. Remember, you can't pour from an empty cup. Prioritizing self-care and setting professional boundaries ensures that you can continue to offer the best support to your clients.

Congratulations on reaching the end of this guide! You're now equipped with comprehensive knowledge, practical strategies, and tools to guide your first client through their initial 90-day recovery journey. The path may be challenging, but the rewards are profound. Every step your client takes towards recovery, every small victory they achieve, every positive change they make, is a testament to your support and dedication.

As you continue this journey, remember — you are making a difference. Here's to you and the transformative work you do!

CONTINUOUS PROFESSIONAL DEVELOPMENT

CHAPTER 7 QUIZ: SELF-CARE AND PROFESSIONAL BOUNDARIES FOR PRS

1. Why is self-care important for a PRS?

a) To avoid burnout and maintain effectiveness
b) To have time for hobbies
c) To appear professional
d) None of the above

2. What can potentially harm the PRS-client professional relationship

a) Setting work-life boundaries
b) Entering into dual relationships with a client
c) Seeking supervision
d) All of the above

3.1. Why is it important for a PRS to maintain professional boundaries?

aa) It creates a wall between the PRS and the client
b) It prevents burnout, stress, and the risk of ethical issues
c) It makes the PRS seem distant and unapproachable
d) None of the above

CHAPTER 7 QUIZ: SELF-CARE AND PROFESSIONAL BOUNDARIES FOR PRS

4.1. What happens when a PRS enters into dual relationships with a client?

a) It strengthens the PRS-client relationship
b) It can lead to conflicts of interest and harm the professional relationship
c) It makes the PRS more likeable
d) None of the above

5. What is not a recommended self-care practice for a PRS?

a) Ignoring their feelings
b) Setting work-life boundaries
c) Seeking supervision when needed
d) Regularly engaging in relaxing activities

CONTINUOUS PROFESSIONAL DEVELOPMENT

Practical Exercises for YOU and your CLIENT

Peer Exercise: Develop a self-care routine that includes activities for physical, emotional, and social wellbeing. Stick to this routine consistently and notice any changes in your stress levels or overall wellbeing.

Client Exercise: Discuss the importance of self-care with your client. Help them develop their own self-care routine and encourage them to incorporate it into their daily life.

Remember, these exercises are meant to be flexible and adaptable. Tailor them according to your unique needs and the specific needs of your client. The key is to create an engaging, supportive, and empowering environment that fosters growth, learning, and healing.

Ready to take your journey of self-love and recovery to the next level? I'm here to help! If you're interested in a one-on-one session with me, please reach out at PrettyNerdyG@gmail.com. Let's dive deeper into your unique journey and build on the foundation you've started here.

Alternatively, if you're looking for a structured, immersive program, consider signing up for "The AFTA Effect: A 6 Week Self Love Leap Bootcamp". This transformative program will provide you with additional tools, insights, and support to enhance your journey towards self-love and recovery.

Visit www.LetsWRAP.com for more information or check out my Linktree at Linktr.ee/PrettyNerdyG to explore all available resources and offerings.

CONCLUSION

JOURNEYING FORWARD AS A PEER RECOVERY SPECIALIST

As we reach the end of this guide, it's essential to reflect on the journey you've embarked upon as a Peer Recovery Specialist (PRS). The role you've taken on is challenging, fulfilling, and transformative, not only for your client but for you as well. You have the power to change lives, to guide individuals from the darkest points of their lives towards the light of recovery, healing, and renewed self-discovery.

Throughout this guide, we've explored the critical elements of the PRS role, the foundations of trust and understanding, the creation and implementation of a comprehensive 90-day recovery plan, dealing with setbacks, therapeutic techniques, fostering long-term recovery, and maintaining your wellbeing through self-care and professional boundaries. Each chapter has offered actionable strategies and insights to navigate your role effectively and provide the best support to your client.

Let's revisit the key takeaways from each chapter:

1.	Understanding the Role of a Peer Recovery Specialist: Emphasize empathy, patience, active listening, and respect in your role as a PRS. Your personal experiences can be an invaluable source of connection, understanding, and motivation for your clients.
2.	Knowing Your Client: Building Trust and Understanding: Build trust through consistency, empathy, and maintaining confidentiality. Understand your client's background, goals, strengths, and triggers to create a personalized recovery plan.
3.	Creating A Comprehensive 90-Day Plan: Create a dynamic recovery plan focused on clear goals, potential triggers, establishing healthy habits, creating a support network, planning for potential setbacks, regular check-ins, and celebrating progress.
4.	Handling Difficulties and Setbacks in the Early Days: Normalize difficulties and setbacks as part of the recovery process, teach coping strategies, foster resilience, provide ongoing support, and leverage the support network.
5.	Therapeutic Techniques for Effective Recovery: Utilize techniques such as Cognitive Behavioral Therapy (CBT), Mindfulness-Based Techniques, Motivational Interviewing (MI), and Relapse Prevention Techniques to provide your clients with the skills and strategies they need to manage their recovery effectively.
6.	Fostering Long-term Commitment to Recovery: Reinforce the benefits of recovery, encourage lifelong learning, maintain regular check-ins, set new goals, foster a supportive community, and empower your client to strengthen their long-term commitment to recovery.
7.	Self-Care and Professional Boundaries for PRS: Prioritize your self-care and establish clear professional boundaries to maintain your wellbeing and ensure the effectiveness of your support.

Now, as you stand on the precipice of your journey as a PRS, equipped with knowledge, strategies, and a deep understanding of the role, remember that you're not alone. The PRS community is vast and supportive, filled with individuals who share your passion and commitment. Lean on this community for support, guidance, and continual learning.

Lastly, remember to celebrate your achievements. Every step you take in this role, every client you support, every change you facilitate is a testament to your strength, commitment, and dedication. You are making a difference. You are changing lives. You are a beacon of hope and transformation.

Embrace your role as a PRS with open arms and an open heart. Keep learning, keep growing, and keep inspiring. Here's to you and the incredible journey you've embarked upon. Your journey as a PRS is just beginning, and the road ahead is filled with possibilities, transformations, and profound impact.

Continue to walk this path with courage, empathy, and unwavering commitment. The world needs more heroes like you. Let's continue making a difference — one life, one day, one step at a time.

*Bonus Weekly Checklist

Here is a weekly checklist for you, the Peer Recovery Specialist (PRS) to help your client during the first 90 days of recovery. This is meant to serve as a general guide; the specifics may vary based on individual circumstances.

Week 1-2: Laying the Foundation

- Define the PRS role and clarify expectations
- Build rapport and trust with the client.
- Gather information about the client's background, substance use history, triggers, strengths, and goals.
- Introduce the concept of a 90-day plan and start discussing its structure.

Week 3-4: Creating the 90-Day Plan

- Define specific, measurable, achievable, relevant, and time-bound (SMART) recovery goals with the client.
- Identify potential triggers and high-risk situations.
- Discuss and plan for coping strategies.
- Begin the formation of a support network.
- Finalize and document the 90-day recovery plan.

*Bonus Weekly Checklist

Week 5-7: Implementing the Plan

- Begin execution of the 90-day plan.
- Regularly check-in on progress towards goals.
- Adjust plan as necessary based on progress and feedback.
- Teach client mindfulness techniques for stress and craving management.
- Continually reinforce the benefits of recovery.

Week 8-10: Managing Setbacks and Refining Techniques

- Normalize and manage any difficulties or setbacks.
- Revise coping strategies if necessary.
- Reinforce the use of support networks.
- Celebrate progress and victories, no matter how small.
- Introduce and practice basic Cognitive Behavioral Therapy (CBT) techniques for managing negative thought patterns.

*Bonus Weekly Checklist

Week 11-13: Fostering Long-term Commiment

- Discuss the importance of a long-term commitment to recovery.
- Reinforce the benefits of sobriety and the positive changes experienced.
- Develop new long-term recovery goals with the client.
- Reiterate the importance of the support network.
- Recap and review lessons learned and strategies that worked during the 90-day period.

Week 14: Celebrating Progress and Planning Ahead

- Celebrate the completion of the 90-day plan and acknowledge the client's progress and effort.
- Discuss any aspects of the plan that need to continue, cease, or be modified.
- Set new short and long-term goals based on the client's current situation and aspirations.
- Ensure the client feels comfortable and prepared to continue their recovery journey beyond the initial 90-day period.
- Discuss ongoing check-in schedule to monitor progress and provide continued support.

Message from the Author

Congratulations on completing "Recovery Reinvented: The First 90 Days with Your Client as a New PRS." I am sincerely grateful that you've trusted me to be part of your transformative journey as a Peer Recovery Specialist. Your role is both demanding and rewarding, an opportunity to turn lives around. As you step onto this path, remember that challenges are gateways to growth. The wisdom you've gained from this book will be an anchor, guiding your interactions with your clients with grace and understanding. Keep expanding your horizons; draw from every resource, every piece of knowledge, to continue learning and evolving. Your commitment to improvement will reflect in the success of your clients. Be proud of the meaningful change you're initiating. Thank you for being a beacon of hope. Keep shining bright in your mission.

Remember, every hurdle you overcome fuels your growth. Use the insights from this book as a steady compass, guiding your interactions with grace and understanding. And don't stop here—continue learning, continue growing.

Visit www.LetsWRAP.com for more resources and to deepen your expertise in the recovery field. In the spirit of lifelong learning, consider booking me for a workshop or presentation. Together, we can explore this noble path in greater depth, reinforcing your skills, and shaping your role as a beacon of hope. Thank you for your commitment to this cause, and for the incredible impact you're about to make.

Keep shining in your mission!

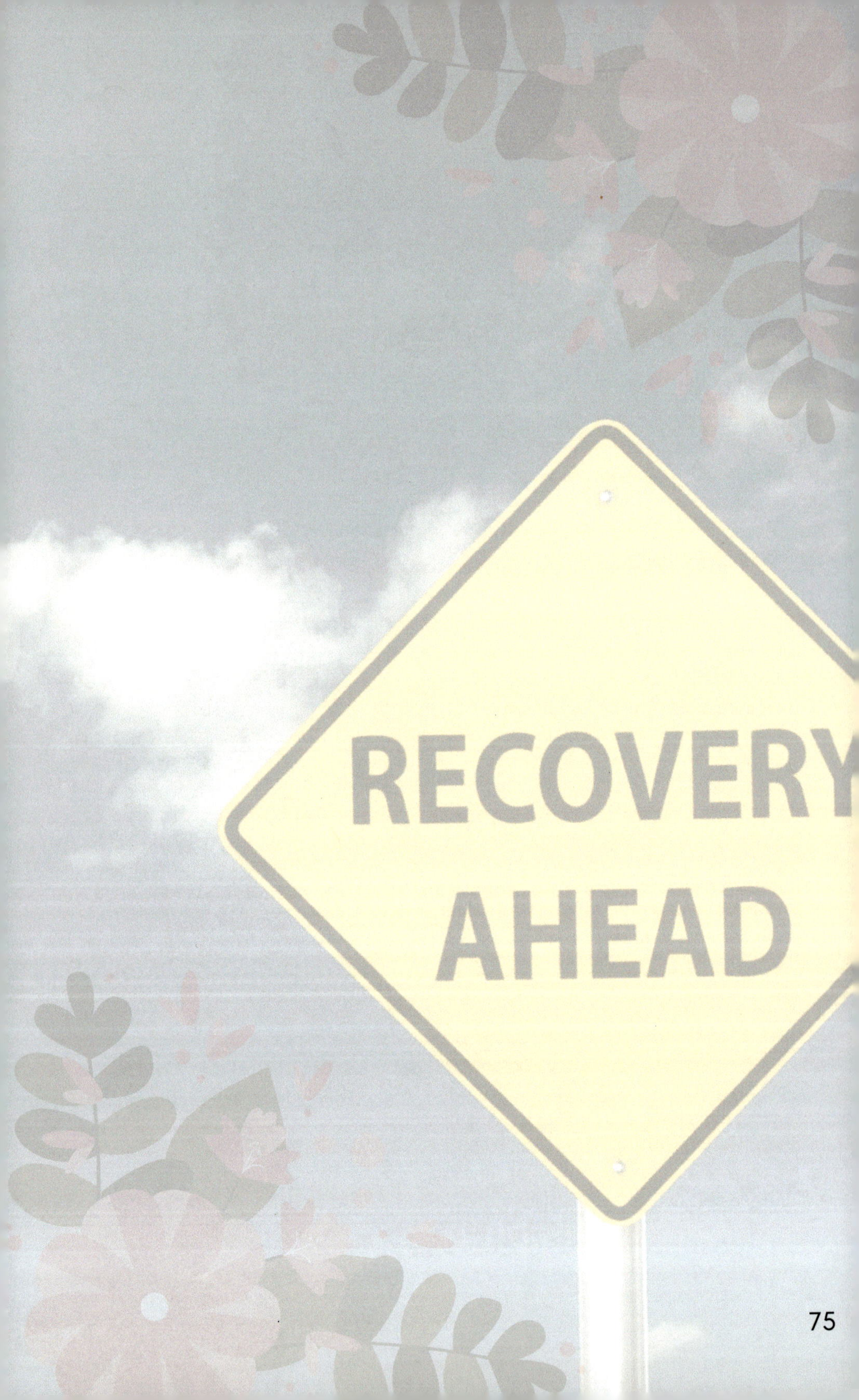
RECOVERY
AHEAD

Recovery Reinvented:

THE FIRST 90 DAYS WITH YOUR CLIENT AS A NEW PRS

RECOVERY AHEAD

Thank You...

It was such a pleasure creating this book. This Book was so awesome to put together because I am so excited to share what I know with people.

My books, courses, workshops and other digital products are all designed for your success, and I can't tell you how important I take each and every one that I create and offer to the public.

I hope you've enjoyed reading it and working through the assignments as much as I enjoyed creating it and I look forward to sharing other Books with you.

I'd love to hear your feedback on how this Book has helped you out. Feel free to reach out and let me know.

Warmly,
Srea Jones-Harrington

Contact Information

Email: PrettyNerdyG@gmail.com
Website: www.LetsWRAP.com

Wanna speak with me in person? Contact me to book your 1 on 1 telephone session TODAY

Made in the USA
Columbia, SC
16 January 2025